On Tracks Broad and Narrow
Fifty Years of Railway Photography

David J. Mitchell

Holne
Publishing

© David J. Mitchell, Ian Drummond & Holne Publishing 2012

British Library Cataloguing in Publication Data
A record for this book is available from the British Library

ISBN 978-0-9563317-3-1
Published by: Holne Publishing, PO Box 343, LEEDS, LS19 9FW
Typeset by: Holne Publishing Services, PO Box 343, LEEDS, LS19 9FW
Printed by: Charlesworth Press, Flanshaw Way, Flanshaw Lane, Wakefeld, WF2 9LP

Photographs in this volume have been digitally adjusted to enhance clarity and also remove blemishes, dust etc. However, no intentional alterations have been made to affect their historical significance.

Changes in place names: For Welsh names modern spellings have been used, for African and other locations place names and spellings contemporaneous with the photograph have been utilised with subsequent changes in brackets.

Maps of locations are indicative only and are not reproduced to a particular scale. North is at the top edge of the map unless otherwise indicated.

KEY FOR MAPS

————	Railway (colour can vary)	••••••••••••	Border between countries or provinces
⬤	Approximate Photo Location	●	Other city/town/station

All photographs copyright David J. Mitchell except photos on pages 33, 38, 53, 55, 64 and 70 which are copyright David J. Mitchell/Colour-Rail. Colour-Rail references: BRW1571, BRW1980, BRM1730, BRM1695, BRE1553 and BRM1779 respectively.
Photographs on pages 12, 15, 39, 41, 42, 45, 46 and 57 are copyright David J. Mitchell/Colour-Rail.

Holne Publishing
PO Box 343
LEEDS
LS19 9FW
enquiries@holnepublishing.co.uk
www.holnepublishing.co.uk

Cover Photos:
Front: *Dukedog* 4-4-0 No.9017 pulls out of Bewdley, on the Severn Valley Railway, with a short freight train on a photographic charter on 14th October 2008. No.9017 was the last *Dukedog* in service and worked the 1960 Talyllyn Railway AGM special between Shrewsbury and Tywyn on September 24th 1960 as its last working. A collection on that train train helped secure its preservation on the Bluebell Railway. It was restored to GWR green livery for one of its first visits away from the Bluebell line.

Back: The engines working in the quarry at Penrhyn were predominantly Hunslet 0-4-0 saddle tanks, but Penrhyn did buy a number of engines second hand. Here *Cegin*, a Barclay 0-4-0 well tank of 1931, bought from the Durham County Water Board in 1936, is working on the cutting shed level hauling a train of waste. Cabs were unusual on Penrhyn quarry-based engines.

A class B1 4-6-0 heads the Bradford portion of a London express up the 1 in 50 climb out of Bradford Exchange on 3rd June 1963. It has just passed St Dunstans where the former Great Northen Railway (GNR) Leeds line swung east, away from the former Lancashire & Yorkshire Railway (L&YR) Halifax line which can be seen in the background. The direct Leeds to Queensbury line diverges to the left and the junction points can be seen alongside the locomotive. The Bradford to London train would normally comprise three coaches and would be attached to the Leeds portion at Wakefield having travelled over the line from Laisterdyke to Ardsley.

Contents

Introduction	5
The Derwent Valley Light Railway	7
The West Riding of Yorkshire	11
Talyllyn Railway	17
The View from the Bridge	21
Mid Wales	24
South Wales	34
Settle & Carlisle and Shap	43
Snow at Dent	52
North East England	56
Scotland	65
The Cromford and High Peak Railway	69
Southern England and the Isle of Wight	71
The West Country	78
Welsh Narrow Gauge in the Sixties	86
Isle of Man	91
Industrial Scenes	99
Austria	103
Portugal	112
East Africa	118
Angola and Nigeria	126
Last Train to Mulobezi	135
Southern Africa	139
Modern Images	147
Shed Scenes	154

From the Series Editor

Starting a new series of books and calling them *Great Railway Photography*, demands that the first in the series be something special. Therefore, I am delighted that David Mitchell, whom I have known for many years due to our mutual involvement with the Talyllyn Railway and whose work I have greatly admired, agreed to provide the first volume in this new series.

The brief I gave David was to choose his favourite photographs from over fifty years of railway photography. This he has done with aplomb with a selection of photographs that covers the end of the steam in Great Britain in the 1960s and the early years of railway preservation, including the Talyllyn Railway, where preservation started. However, David has also given us a perspective on railways in Austria, Portugal and particularly Africa during the late 1960s and early 1970s.

Of course, David has far from 'hung up his camera' and so the story comes into the 21st Century with some stunning shots, many now making use of digital photography, to recreate scenes from the past. As ever I am grateful to those who have offered assistance; to my wife, Di, as well as Lawrie Bowles, Alan Doe, and John and Barbara Plumtree-Varley for their help with proof-reading. I hope that you will agree that this collection is worthy of the title *Great Railway Photography*.

Ian Drummond

Left: This one counts as 'Editor's choice', as it is simply one of the best photos of an Isle of Wight class O2 I have seen. W16 *Ventnor* stands at Ryde Esplanade with a train for Cowes on 18th December 1962. In the background a tramcar can be seen in the tram terminus.

Introduction

This collection of pictures has been taken over the past fifty years or so and has been selected to bring back memories of happy times. I was introduced to railways, both full size and model, at an early age. My grandfather was interested in both and we often went to see trains in various places. He liked express trains and we picnicked in a field at Alne alongside the East Coast Main Line while watching Gresley Pacifics at speed, as well as the occasional train on the Easingwold Railway.

Another regular location was Bingley, where we went most Saturday afternoons. We had tea and toasted teacake in the Loft Café, where grandfather enjoyed a free read of the owner's copy of *Autocar* and then went to the station. In school holidays we would go riding on trains in the area and also go to Leeds to ride on the trams.

An introduction to the Talyllyn Railway (TR), and to the Railway Correspondence and Travel Society (RCTS), resulted in widening horizons with more opportunities to see steam at work. Later still, working in Africa in the 1970s also provided an opportunity to see some of the interesting railways on that continent. Highlights of my time there included riding the last Zambezi Sawmills Railway (ZSR) train from Mulobezi and visiting Angola. The sight of a wood burning Garratt working hard at night is unforgettable, but also impossible to record, at least with the equipment I had.

Above: My first ride on a locomotive. The trip David Barraclough and I did on the Derwent Valley Light Railway (DVLR) in 1958 was our first trip on a minor railway. The DVLR with its grass grown track was very different from the railways I had known and the highlight was travelling on the engine from Cliffe Common back to York. No.65714 was a British Railways (BR) engine on hire to the DVLR, which had nearly always hired its motive power from the North Eastern Railway (NER), as well as its successors the London and North Eastern Railway (LNER) and BR. In this case No.65714 was an ex-LNER class J25 built at Darlington in 1900 and withdrawn in January 1961. David and I each had our picture taken in the cab before leaving Cliffe Common.

Right: Interest in transport generally as well as railways resulted in pictures being taken of buses, trolleybuses and trams, including some oddities like the chain ferry across Blyth harbour. The steam worked vessel pulled itself across the harbour on two cables anchored at each side, which normally lay on the seabed when the ferry was at either shore, allowing ships to pass. This ferry connected the town of Blyth on the south side of the harbour with the quays and industry on the north side. It was introduced in 1890, though the vessel shown was introduced later and was withdrawn in 1964, being replaced by a motor ferry. It is seen here on 8th February 1964.

Although described as fifty years of railway photography this is a slight misnomer as the twenty-five years from the late 1970s are omitted. Not because I did not take pictures, but because of space limitations. My interest also extended beyond railways to trams, trolleybuses and even buses. Canals and ships were also photographed, but in this selection only the odd tram and ferry are featured. Therefore, these pictures are a brief look at areas and railways which I enjoyed, and as such they are very much a potpourri.

The modern section features the preservation scene and shows how the seeds sown by Tom Rolt and the early pioneers on the Talyllyn have blossomed into restored railways and rebuilt rolling stock. This is the result of the efforts of thousands of volunteers, recreating sights and sounds of a somewhat rose-tinted past. Others have no doubt travelled more widely, and taken better photographs, but if this collection brings as much pleasure to the reader as taking the pictures has brought to me, it will make it all worthwhile.

I am grateful to Ian for suggesting this book and for his efforts to ensure the quality of the pictures. Unfortunately, I did not keep copious notes about times and locations and, as a result, any errors in the captions are mine.

My thanks are also due to all those who helped make the trips possible and enjoyable, as well as those who have helped clarify details relating to the pictures. They are too numerous to name individually, but I thank them all. Finally my wife Janet for support and understanding during many years and on numerous trips.

Left: Bradford City Passenger Transport (BCPT) tramways became the final 4 ft gauge tramway to close when the last trams ran to Odsal on 6th May 1950. In my childhood we lived at Undercliffe which was served by trams until July 1948. The route had been closed in 1935 being replaced by buses, but the trams were reinstated at the outbreak of war. Going into town I would insist we went on the tram, riding on the open balcony, despite the conductor telling mother there would be a bus before the tram left.

No.104 was the official decorated last car and, with official indifference to preserving a tram, the Bradford Northern Rugby Club planned to acquire No.104 and display it, decorations and all, at Odsal Stadium. However, confusion intervened and it was stripped to a bare body. When the tram body finally arrived at the stadium it was used as a scoreboard. A change of management at BCPT, and the activity of a group of enthusiasts, led to the body being recovered.

With the active assistance of Thornbury works it was mounted on a regauged former Sheffield truck, and, painted in the 1938 style, returned to operational condition. It ran occasionally on the track still remaining at Thornbury depot, using the trolleybus positive overhead. Here it is seen at the Leeds Road end of the works approach on 14th September 1963 on its last public 'excursion'. It is now in the Industrial Museum at Moorside Mills with trolleybus No.737.

The Derwent Valley Light Railway

I first saw the Derwent Valley Light Railway (DVLR) when we went to visit friends in Hornsea in the school holidays and crossed the grass grown track east of Selby. Intrigued, I found out what it was and duly wrote to ask if we could ride on the line. We could and Mr. Reading, the general manager, did not seem concerned when two 15 year old lads arrived at Layerthorpe station in York to ride on the daily freight to Cliffe Common. One of last light railways, opening in 1913, the passenger service ceased in 1926 and it remained independent at Nationalisation. The closure of the Selby to Market Weighton line in 1964 deprived the DVLR of its southern outlet, and the line was cut back in stages until the last train to Dunnington ran on 27th September 1981.

Though the passenger service had ceased in 1926 there were a number of enthusiast specials run over the line. On 27th September 1963 a joint RCTS/Stephenson Locomotive Society (SLS) five day tour of the North East started at York and travelled over the DVLR to Cliffe Common, continuing via Harrogate, Skipton & Carlisle to Newcastle that day. Hauled by Ivatt 2-6-0 No.46409 it is seen entering Dunnington, where there was a photographic stop.

The train travelled slowly over the DVLR enabling us to chase it by car. Here it is seen entering Cliffe Common station, where it would regain BR tracks. There was a look of relief on the faces of the crew when they got back on the main line. We continued chasing the train and a picture of it on the Settle & Carlisle will be found on page 46.

Left: For much of its life the DVLR hired motive power from the main line company, North Eastern Railway (NER), London and North Eastern Railway (LNER) & BR. By about 1960 steam was replaced by a diesel shunter, usually a class 03. Here a southbound train is seen approaching Wheldrake station hauled by D2112 on 21st July 1964. The signal, which was the only one on the line, was linked to the crossing gates to indicate if they were open as visibility was limited by the curve and a cutting, one of the few earthworks on the line.

Right: D2112 shunting in Wheldrake yard on 21st July 1964; the grass grown state of the track is obvious. The six-wheeled van was built for the South Eastern and Chatham Railway (SECR) in 1905 and is now preserved at the Bluebell Railway. In the background is the water tank, the only watering point other than Layerthorpe.

In 1976 the DVLR sought to benefit from steam railway tourism, and the opening of the National Railway Museum (NRM) in York, by introducing a tourist train. *Joem*, a J72 NER design 0-6-0T, which carried the number 69023 in BR service, along with a couple of coaches, were obtained and a service introduced between York (Layerthorpe) and Dunnington. It was not a success and ceased in 1979. Here *Joem* stands at Layerthorpe with the once daily train on 18th May 1977. The building immediately to the right of the engine is the DVLR head office.

The West Riding

The West Riding of Yorkshire was my home area. Here there was a fascinating network of railways and trains varied from the East Coast expresses from Kings Cross to Leeds and Bradford, the Midland line trains like the *Thames Clyde*, the transpennine routes and the smaller lines. These latter lines were often heavily engineered and served by trains with a couple of coaches and a tank engine. In the industrialised areas the stations were usually soot-blackened and often still gas-lit.

West Riding Locations

The former Great Northern (GNR) station in Leeds was the slightly misnamed Leeds Central. It was the terminus of the expresses and graced with A4s as well as lesser engines. Steam finished on the London trains in 1963 and here an express from London has arrived at Leeds Central hauled by DP2, one of the prototype diesels, on 18th February 1967 a couple of months before the station closed. A little later DP2 worked the Bradford portion of the *Yorkshire Pullman* from Leeds to Bradford. DP2 was wrecked on 31st July 1967 near Thirsk when it hit derailed wagons from a down freight on the adjacent slow line, and was damaged beyond repair.

Class B1 No.61129 pulls empty stock out of Leeds Central station on 30th September 1963. The coaches had arrived from London behind A4 No.60006 *Sir Ralph Wedgwood* and would be taken to Copley Hill sidings for servicing.

Jubilee class No.45565 *Victoria* based at Low Moor shed, was one of the last *Jubilees* in service. At Whitsuntide 1966 it is seen leaving Bradford Exchange on an excursion to Blackpool, starting up the 1 in 50 gradient to Bowling Junction. The station was operated as two units. The former Lancashire and Yorkshire (L&YR) traffic for Halifax and Manchester on the left and the former GNR traffic to Leeds and London on the right. It closed in 1973 to be replaced by Bradford Interchange, a little to the south, with the result that the buffer stops are now where the signal box stood and the bridge has been replaced by an embankment.

Queensbury was the point at which the former GNR lines from Bradford to Keighley and Halifax diverged. It was a triangular station with platforms on all three sides. Over a mile from, and 400 ft below, Queensbury village local traffic was quickly lost to the electric tramways from Bradford and Halifax. The passenger service was withdrawn in 1955 and the line to Holmfield through Queensbury tunnel closed. Freight continued to Cullingworth and Thornton on the Keighley line until 25th June 1965. In October 1962 2-6-2T No. 41282 propelled an inspection saloon up the line from Bradford and it is seen in the Halifax platform. The Keighley line ran behind the station building which was at the eastern apex of the triangle. From here the train then pulled back to the points and proceeded to Thornton before returning to Bradford.

The Calder Valley line had running loops between Mytholmroyd and Luddendenfoot. Former L&YR A class No.52121 potters along the eastbound loop with a rake of empty wagons on 27th September 1962, shortly before its withdrawal in November 1962.

The branch from Embsay Junction, just outside Skipton on the Ilkley line, to Grassington was a latecomer, being opened in 1902. Passenger services ceased in 1930 as the station at Grassington was too far from the village, but the freight service continued to Grassington until 1969 and it became the last steam-worked branch line on BR. Freight trains still serve the lime works at Swinden, 1½ miles south of Grassington. On 26th March 1964 Class 4F No.44468 heads the freight from Grassington through the former station at Rylstone. The level crossing is guarded by a Midland Railway (MR) signal in the Grassington direction, but the other signal, off in the picture, has a London and North Western Railway arm. No.44468 is fitted with a tender cab.

Talyllyn Railway

As a young lad I was taken to the Talyllyn Railway (TR) on a Yorkshire Area working party at Easter 1959 by the late John Halliday. As they say, the rest is history and I have been involved with the TR ever since, including a stint as Managing Director.

Though much has changed over the years there is a timelessness about the TR as the train makes its way up the Fathew Valley. The original carriages are still in regular use and the two original TR locos have been overhauled and are still in daily service.

Talyllyn Railway Location

Right: At 8.30 am on 27th July 1963 the locomotives are being prepared for the days work outside Pendre shed. The shed is almost certainly the oldest continuously used steam locomotive shed in the world having been built in 1867. On the left is No.4 *Edward Thomas*, built by Kerr Stuart in 1921 for the neighbouring Corris Railway. That line closed in 1948 and the two surviving locomotives, Nos. 3 & 4, remained sheeted up in the narrow gauge yard at Machynlleth. They were probably the only two locomotives in the world to fit the Talyllyn's 2 ft 3 in gauge, as well as its very restricted loading gauge, and so they were bought by the Talyllyn Railway Preservation Society (TRPS) in March 1951. At the shed door is No.2 *Dolgoch*, built for the TR by Fletcher Jennings in 1866. It had been the only workable locomotive since about 1945 and worked the 1951 service, the first year of preservation, on its own. It was sent away for major rebuilding, including a new boiler in 1954 and had just returned the previous month so I made a special day trip to Tywyn to see it. On the right is No.6 *Douglas*, built by Andrew Barclay in 1918 for the Air Service Construction Corps as their No.1. It later worked at RAF Calshot and was then bought by Abelson and Co. for possible resale to India. This fell through and the locomotive was given to the TR by Abelson, and was regauged from 2 ft to 2 ft 3 in by Hunt Brothers, arriving in Tywyn in 1954.

Again on 27th July 1963 No.4 stands at Wharf Station with the 10.25 am train to Abergynolwyn. The train comprises No.9, one of the two bogie coaches built with softwood bodies on mine car chassis at Pendre. The tendency of the hardboard panels to distort led to them being referred to as the 'cardboard carriages'. Two of 1866 Brown Marshall carriages are followed by a carriage from the erstwhile Glyn Valley Tramway (GVT). Rescued from a field, it was restored and finished in the GVT green and cream livery and fitted out as a first class carriage. The 1866 brake van brings up the rear. No.4 has the *Giesl* ejector chimney fitted in 1958. In the background is the Narrow Gauge Railway Museum and outside piles of blocks for the extension that would shortly be built.

Rapidly growing traffic in the late 1960s led to the decision to rebuild Abergynolwyn station and also to introduce a three-train set peak service. Previously the two train sets had crossed at Brynglas, but for three trains additional loops were required to enable a suitable timetable to be operated. The loop at Pendre was upgraded to allow passenger trains to cross and a new loop installed at Quarry Siding. Here at Easter 1969 the formation at Quarry has been levelled and the west end point has been installed. No.4 *Edward Thomas* heads a down train comprising some of the new bogie coaches, which started to appear in the 1960s using commercially-built body shells. These were mounted on chassis and fitted out at Pendre. No.4 has had its conventional chimney replaced after the *Giesl* ejector plating wore thin.

At Abergynolwyn the TRPS sold basic refreshments from the small enclosed end of the station building. This became unsatisfactory and the Chief Engineer, John Bate, conceived the idea of a 'Tea Van'. This he built on a chassis that had been under one of the former Penrhyn open coach bodies which had been withdrawn. A siding was installed at Abergynolwyn and the Tea Van came up at the front of the first up train. Here it is is being shunted onto the siding by No.6 *Douglas*. The side flaps on the van will then be opened and the refreshments served over the counter inside. During the winter of 1968/9 the station was rebuilt and the new building included refreshment facilities. However, the Tea Van then found further service as the mess van for the gangs upgrading the extension to Nant Gwernol.

The View From The Bridge

Neptune Road bridge in Tywyn, south of the main line station and adjacent to the Talyllyn station, has been the vantage point for many pictures of the main line trains over the years. This scene has changed with the growth of trees to the south and the more recent installation of steel fencing. The main line station has lost its goods yard and the site is now the Co-op supermarket. At the station the footbridge has also gone and passengers now use a pedestrian crossing.

Right: The down goods shunting at Tywyn station in November 1964. Unusually double-headed by 2-6-4T 4MT No.80098 and No.2236, a Collett 0-6-0. Part of the train has been left on the down main whilst the engines shunt into the yard on the up side.

Looking south from the bridge standard class 3MT 2-6-2T No.82020 runs into Tywyn with a Machynlleth to Pwllheli afternoon train on 11th July 1964. In the background is the wharf at the Talyllyn station. Some TR engineering wagons are on the wharf edge track, including three hopper wagons obtained from the Winchburgh Shale railway in Scotland. During preservation days the wharf siding was used for receipt of coal and rail and the despatch of scrap. The occasional TR engine going on tour by rail also used the siding for loading onto a standard gauge wagon.

From 1953 to 1982 the TRPS ran a special train from London to Tywyn in connection with the Society AGM and a wide variety of engines were used over the years. The train usually ran via Welshpool, but in 1954, and between 1962 to 1964, the train ran via Ruabon and Dolgellau, reversing at Ruabon and Morfa Mawddach (Barmouth Junction). On 26th September 1964 the train was hauled from Ruabon by No.7827 *Lydham Manor* and prairie tank No.4555. This latter engine had been bought by Pat Whitehouse and Pat Garland (Secretary and Treasurer of the TRPS respectively) and painted in GWR livery. Here the empty stock is leaving Tywyn for Machynlleth for servicing before the overnight journey back to London, which would leave Tywyn about 11.30 pm.

Mid Wales

My involvement with the Talyllyn Railway led to visiting the various lines in Wales, especially the former Cambrian Railways and Great Western Railway (GWR) routes in Mid Wales. These were long single lines through attractive but often remote countryside. Happily the coast line from Machynlleth to Pwllheli is still with us and, until recently, had steam trains in summer.

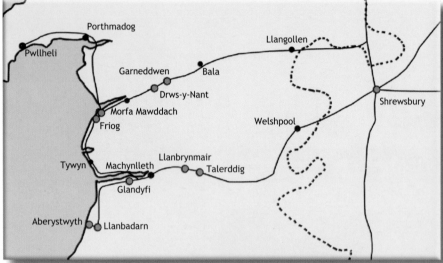

Map of Mid Wales Locations

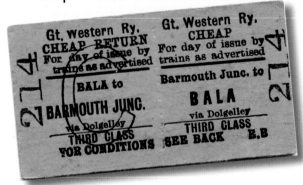

Right: Class 4MT No.75033 heads the last up *Cambrian Coast Express* out of Talerddig cutting on 4th March 1967. The front headboard and other embellishments had been applied by a group of enthusiasts at Aberystwyth station to ensure Cambrian steam went out in style. Later the name reappeared on some trains, but this was the end of the Paddington to Aberystwyth service.

South from Aberystwyth was the line to Carmarthen, formerly the Manchester and Milford Railway which led a hand-to-mouth existence from its opening in 1864 until its takeover by the GWR in 1909. Serving a very sparsely populated area the service was mainly three trains daily in each direction. Here No.7827 *Lydham Manor* heads its three coach train out of Aberystwyth on the 56 mile, 2½ hour journey, in the late afternoon on the last southbound train of the day on 10th June 1964. Aberystwyth shed is in the background, which is now used by the Vale of Rheidol Railway, and the raised area of the coal stage has been levelled. *Lydham Manor* has been preserved and is based at the Paignton and Dartmouth Steam Railway.

Cambrian Coast Expresses were the last steam workings on the Cambrian lines. The portion from Pwllheli had ceased on 3rd September 1966, but the Aberystwyth train continued until March 1967. Class 4MT No.75048 heads the up Express approaching Llanbadarn on a crisp morning on 11th February 1967. Between Aberystwyth and Llanbadarn the line had been double track and the remains of the former down line are visible. On the extreme left can be seen the track of the Vale of Rheidol Railway.

No.7819 *Hinton Manor* heads the Aberystwyth portion of the up *Cambrian Coast Express* through Glandyfi en-route to Dovey Junction, half a mile further north, where it was allowed six minutes to attach the coaches from Pwllheli before continuing with the train to Shrewsbury on 13th July 1964. *Hinton Manor* has also been preserved by the Severn Valley Railway Rolling Stock Trust.

On the line from Shrewsbury to Machynlleth the gradient eased through Llanbrynmair, providing momentary relief for up trains climbing to Talerddig Summit. Here No.7803 *Barcote Manor* is steaming well with the up *Cambrian Coast Express* heading to Shrewsbury on 30th May 1964, as the signalman watches the token exchange. A Gresley coach leads the Pwllheli portion with the coaches from Aberystwyth at the rear. The white buffers were still pristine when the engine returned with the down train from Shrewsbury later in the day.

Shrewsbury is very much a focal point for Mid Wales, and, with the closure of the Cambrian main line north of Welshpool, has become the starting point for the remaining Cambrian lines. No.1016 *County of Hants* stands at Shrewsbury with a Chester to Birmingham train on 1st August 1962. The station still had its overall roof and side screens.

North of Tywyn the Pwllheli line stayed close to the coast. Here on 26th September 1964 the TRPS AGM special from Paddington via Ruabon to Tywyn heads south from the avalanche tunnel at Friog, high above Cardigan Bay with Barmouth in the background, after reversing at Morfa Mawddach. The train is headed by *Manor* class No.7827 *Lydham Manor* and Prairie tank No.4555.

Morfa Mawddach, Barmouth Junction until 1960, was one of those remote junctions where trains connected, but at least it had road access unlike Dovey and Bala Junctions. Here the line from Ruabon joined the Cambrian Coast line from Machynlleth to Pwllheli. A class 2MT heads a Dolgellau to Barmouth local from the Ruabon line platforms out onto Barmouth viaduct on 26th September 1964.

The Morfa Mawddach to Ruabon line was scheduled to close on 16th January 1965. However, serious flooding in Mid Wales washed out an embankment east of Llandderfel on 12th December 1964 and buses were substituted between Bala and Llangollen. Ivatt class 2 2-6-0 No.46446 runs into Drws-y-Nant with a Barmouth to Bala train on the frosty morning of 19th December 1964 on the climb from Dolgellau to Garneddwen summit. Gavin Morrison has taken his picture and stands by the gate ready for a quick getaway.

Some swift driving enabled us to photograph the same train, with No.46446, breasting the summit before passing under the A494 and entering the loop and halt at Garneddwen. The fields are frost covered but the sun had come out making for a memorable scene. Note that the signal arms for Garneddwen loop have been removed.

South Wales

The railway network in South Wales was very complex with some valleys having multiple lines. By the 1960s much of the duplication had gone and the valley lines from Cardiff were operated by DMUs. However, steam remained on freight and on the various lines linking across the main valley lines, as well as on the railways heading north from the valleys to the rural areas beyond the Brecon Beacons. Many of the lines were steeply-graded and much of the traffic was worked by tank engines.

Map of South Wales Locations

Left: Pontypool Road trains started from the up platform at Neath General station. No.4157, a regular performer on the line at this time, waits to depart on 21st September 1963. Shortly after leaving the station it will swing right onto the Vale of Neath line. The DMU in the centre road is a SLS Special, touring various branches in the Neath and Swansea area.

Abercynon on the Cardiff to Merthyr line is the junction for Aberdare. Looking north a Cardiff to Aberdare DMU heads onto the branch whilst No.5622, a Collett 0-6-2T comes off the Aberdare line with a brake van in tow on 20th September 1963. On the right the Merthyr line climbs steeply up to Quaker's Yard (Low Level).

Right: A morning Neath to Pontypool Road train leaving Hengoed (High Level) and crossing Hengoed viaduct on 20th September 1963, headed by a Collett designed 2-6-2T 51XX, introduced in 1929. The railings in the foreground are on the platform of the former Brecon & Merthyr Railway Maesycwmmer station, which had closed to passengers on 31st December 1962.

Opposite: Also on 20th September 1963, at Quaker's Yard, the Neath to Pontypool Road line crossed the Taff Valley and the Cardiff to Merthyr lines. West of Quaker's Yard (High Level) the line was single across the valley and through the tunnel into the adjoining Dare Valley. No.6847 *Tidmarsh Grange* waits with a west-bound freight whilst an unidentified 56XX, 0-6-2T arrives with a Neath to Pontypool Road train.

Nearer the eastern end of the Neath to Pontypool Road line at Crumlin it crossed the Ebbw Valley on a massive lattice viaduct, which was the highest railway viaduct in the United Kingdom. Crumlin (High Level) station was at the western end of the viaduct. The track over the viaduct had been singled to avoid the risk of two trains being on the structure at once. Here a Neath-bound train runs into the station hauled by No.4157, a 2-6-2T, on 20th September 1963, but sadly the passenger service ceased on 13th June 1964.

An eastbound coal train heads out of Crumlin (High Level) onto the viaduct on 20th September 1963. Double-heading was not allowed over the viaduct which can be seen above the banking engine, an 0-6-0PT. The viaduct was 200 ft high and was closed completely in June 1964, being demolished the following year. At the far end of the viaduct is Crumlin Junction where a connecting line went down to join the Ebbw Vale line at Llanhilleth.

The former Brecon & Merthyr Railway service ran from Newport to Brecon and it crossed the Beacons with a summit at Torpantau at 1,313 ft. Passenger services ceased on 31st December 1962, but freight continued to run from Merthyr to Brecon until 4th May 1964. No.9776 0-6-0PT leaves Talybont on Usk heading south on 20th September 1963 at the start of the seven mile climb to Torpantau summit and is about to cross the Monmouthshire and Brecon canal.

Halfway up the 1 in 38 bank from Talybont was the passing loop and halt at Pentir Rhiw. Here 0-6-0PT No.4679 takes water at the halt on 28th July 1962, working the 12.10 pm Brecon to Newport train. It was allowed 29 minutes for the seven mile climb. At the bottom right of the picture is the runaway siding. Down trains were brought to a stand before the points were reset to allow them to continue down the bank. In the background is the Talybont Reservoir.

Further down the line with the Brecon Beacons and the Taff Fechan reservoir in the background, No.9776 leaves Pontsticill Junction on 20th September 1963 heading to Morlais Junction and Merthyr. To the right of the building the Newport line climbs away to Dowlais Top. That route, as far as Pant, is now used by the Brecon Mountain Railway and their trains run along the side of the reservoir towards Torpantau.

Settle & Carlisle and Shap

The high fells around Ais Gill and Shap provided superb scenery for photography as well as the sight and sound of trains working hard, although it must be added also a lot of wet and cloudy weather. The Settle & Carlisle (S&C) with its massive engineering works and wilder scenery is probably my favourite line. My first experience of the S&C was with a railtour with preserved Midland compound No.1000. What better introduction! Steam remained on the two lines until the end of 1967, and we made numerous visits in weather both fair and foul.

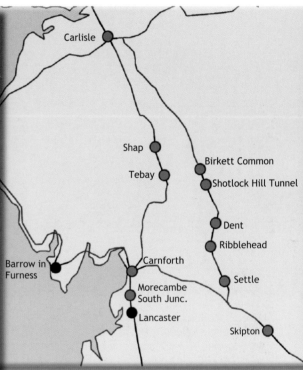

Map of Locations

Ribblehead Viaduct is the iconic structure on the S&C. On a sunny day a *Jubilee* heads the down *Waverley* on 25th August 1962 over the viaduct towards the Blea Moor distant signal. In the background is Pen-y-Ghent.

Below: The same day, after photographing No.123 at Tebay, we travelled home to Halifax via Dent where Black Five No.45105 was heading an up freight through the station shortly after a heavy rain shower.

Above: An unusual visitor at Tebay on 9th September 1963 is Caledonian Railway single wheeler, No.123. It had stopped for water on its journey south from Scotland to work a special from London to the Bluebell Railway on 15th September, piloting preserved London and South Western Railway T9 No.120. No.123 was one of four Scottish engines restored to working order in the late 1950s, which worked railtours and special trains until the mid 1960s. Note the thistles engraved on the front buffer heads.

Britannia class No.70006 *Robert Burns* storms into Dent with a down fitted freight on a rather hazy day, 18th January 1964. The remains of the wooden snow fencing is visible on the hillside above the track.

27th September 1963 started with following the class 2 2-6-0 on the RCTS/SLS railtour on the Derwent Valley Light Railway (see pages 7 & 8) and ended with this view of the same train, now hauled by No.46238 *City of Carlisle* leaving Shotlock Hill tunnel, just south of Ais Gill summit. The picture is slightly fraudulent as the train comprised of only five coaches. No.46238 had taken over the train at Skipton for the run to Carlisle. After taking this shot we drove to Tywyn for the TRPS AGM.

We probably spent far too much time on the southern side of Ais Gill, but the northern climb had some fine scenery and here a class 8F toils up past Birkett Common with an up freight. Leaking steam, it was making heavy weather of the climb in November 1967.

Hughes Crab No.42777 enters Upperby yard, Carlisle with a down freight after what looks to have been a wet journey over Shap on 5th October 1963. The wide array of tracks which were around the railway in steam days are something which has largely disappeared from the railway scene today.

Not strictly Shap; a scruffy ex-War Department 2-8-0 No.90681 trundles through the high-level tracks at Carnforth on a Barrow-bound freight off the Skipton line in August 1964.

No.46240 *City of Coventry* approaches Morecambe South Junction under clear signals with a train for Perth in August 1964.

A dirty Black Five heads a very mixed parcels train, including a mail coach as second vehicle, past Shap Wells with a Stanier 2-6-4T banking on a clear, cold winter's day in December 1964.

Snow at Dent

During the winter of 1962/3 the Settle & Carlisle was badly affected by snow and was closed for various periods, traffic being diverted via Ingleton. Dent station, some 1,100 ft above sea level and reached via a steep and twisty lane, was not the easiest of places to get to but I managed two visits with various friends.

My first visit was on 5th January 1963 with Keith Walton. It was a dull overcast day with some snow flurries. Here the relief up *Thames Clyde Express* passes Dent station leaving a trail of smoke and the background is totally obscured. Sadly I failed to note the engine number.

The second visit was made on 26th January 1963 with Gavin Morrison and it was a lovely sunny day. The line had been closed for several days previously and only re-opened that day. Here the up *Waverley* passes the site of one of the drifts which had blocked the line. It is headed by class A3 No.60073 *St Gatien* between Rise Hill tunnel and the cutting north of Dent station.

There was a steady procession of trains that day as traffic was cleared, and here Black Five No.44674 heads another northbound freight into Dent, photographed from the signal box steps. The more open nature of the line south of the station had reduced drifting.

Viewed from the same spot as the photo on page 52, on the road crossing the line north of the station on 26th January 1963, Black Five No.44669 heads a northbound freight through the station. My yellow Mini stands in the station yard. Going down the hill from Dent station was interesting as any attempt to use the engine for braking resulted in the back end overtaking the front, a problem with front wheel drive.

North East England

The north east of England was predominantly served by the lines of the former North Eastern Railway (NER). The NER was one of the major pre-grouping English companies which did not serve London. Its lines and stations were generally well built and had a solid and permanent air. The routes served the industrial areas, the Pennine Dales and the East Coast. Some of my earliest railway recollections are of the lines in the Harrogate area, including exploring the remains of the Nidd Valley Light Railway.

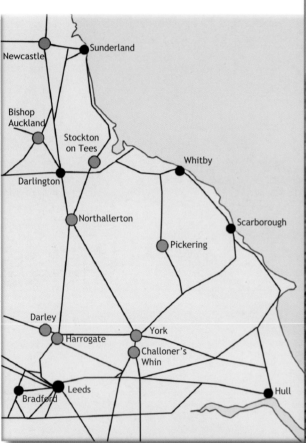

Map of North East England
Locations

The Q6 class 0-8-0s were one of the most successful NER classes and lasted almost until the end of steam. A heavy freight locomotive, No.63417 is not overtaxed with a light engineering train heading north towards Harrogate, near Rigton Lane, on the Leeds to Northallerton line on the lovely spring morning of 11th March 1964.

The branch from Harrogate to Pateley Bridge up the Nidd Valley had lost its passenger service in 1951, but freight continued until 30th October 1964. Here class K1 No.62046 approaches Darley hauling a lightweight train back from Pateley Bridge on 11th March 1964. Interestingly the open wagon does not appear to be piped and the hopper wagon is behind the brake van.

York station with its curved overall roof is one of the most imposing station structures. Newly preserved A4 No.4498 *Sir Nigel Gresley* heads a London to Newcastle railtour slowly through the (now lifted) centre tracks at York on 23rd July 1967.

South of York, the line to Selby and London used to diverge from the Leeds and Sheffield line at Challoner's Whin Junction before the Selby avoiding line was built. On 31st August 1963 an unusually clean WD 2-8-0, No.90449, heads a coal train southwards down the Leeds and Sheffield line. The cottages are typical NER staff housing, whilst the garage is 1950s prefab style.

On 13th April 1964 *The Great Marquess* worked a special train from Leeds to Whitby for the making of a BBC programme about preserved locomotives. Here the special is entering Pickering from Malton whilst B1 No.61021 shunts in the goods yard. Pickering is now the southern terminus of the North Yorkshire Moors Railway, but sadly the line between Pickering and Malton (Rillington Junction) closed to passengers on 6th March 1965 and to all traffic on 1st July 1966.

Newly-preserved by the late Alan Pegler, class A3 No.4472 *Flying Scotsman* starts away from Northallerton with a private special, consisting of Pullman cars and the Devon Belle observation car on 10th April 1965. The train was run to thank those at Darlington Works who had overhauled No.4472 and restored it to its earlier appearance without smoke deflectors.

Class A4 No.60004 *William Whitelaw* on an RCTS special from Leeds to the Newcastle area. In the fading light the train takes on water at Stockton prior to the run back to Leeds via York on 19th September 1965.

Bishop Auckland was once the centre of a network of lines and was one of the few triangular stations. On 10th April 1965 class K4 2-6-0 *The Great Marquess*, privately owned by Viscount Garnock and restored as LNER No.3442, heads north over the Wear Viaduct en route to Durham with an RCTS railtour.

At Manors, just north of Newcastle, a class V3 2-6-2T No.67684 heads an empty stock train en route to Heaton on 8th February 1964. The overhead wires are for the electric locomotives which worked the quayside branch.

Scotland

Eyemouth is a small fishing port just north of Berwick, which was served by a three mile branch from Burnmouth on the East Coast main line. No.64917 is a class J39 0-6-0, a Gresley-designed locomotive introduced in 1927. It is not going to be overtaxed with its one coach train to Burnmouth on 22nd July 1961. Behind the loco the brake composite coach carried a roofboard EYEMOUTH - BURNMOUTH. The line closed on 5th February 1962.

No.55173, an ex-Caledonian Railway 0-4-4T built in 1900, stands at Killin with its train of one coach and a van for Killin Junction where it will connect with trains on the Callander to Oban (C&O) line on 31st July 1961. The Killin branch opened in 1886 and was worked by the Caledonian, becoming part of the London Midland and Scottish Railway (LMS) in 1923. The line extended a further mile beyond Killin to Loch Tay, where it connected with steamers on the Loch until 1939 when the passenger service beyond Killin ceased, although the line remained for access to the little loco shed there. There was no loop at Killin and the coach was run down by gravity while the loco went into the siding. Killin Junction was purely an interchange point and described in the timetable as 'Exchange Platform only'. The line was scheduled to close, together with the C&O between Dunblane and Crianlarich, on 1st November 1965, but a massive landslide in Glen Ogle, just east of Killin junction, on 27th September closed the line prematurely.

A joint RCTS/SLS three day railtour started at Perth on 14th June 1962 and went to Inverness, Kyle of Lochalsh as well as Wick and Thurso, having been planned as the last steam workings north of Inverness. The first day was Perth to Kyle and back to Inverness. From Inverness the train was worked by Black Five No.44978, which is seen here leaving Kyle shed for the return trip to Inverness. There have been other steam specials to Kyle, but No.44978 was probably the last to use the turntable and shed.

Inverness shed was in a rather derelict condition on 16th June 1962 when preserved Highland Railway (HR) No.103 was seen on the turntable at the roundhouse. Built in 1894 it was withdrawn and preserved in 1934, being painted in HR green livery in 1935. In 1959 it was restored to working order and painted in what was described as the Stroudley yellow livery thought to be the livery in which at least some of the 'Big Goods' engines first appeared. Two days earlier it had worked the railtour from Perth to Inverness piloted by preserved Great North of Scotland Railway No. 49 *Gordon Highlander,* and the previous day, having worked light engine to Georgemas Junction, had worked the railtour from there to Thurso and Wick and back to Inverness. On this day it would work light engine to Aviemore, with No.49 and then take the railtour, which had worked over the old line via Forres, on to Aberdeen via the Spey Valley line. Withdrawn again in 1966 it is now on display in the new Riverside Museum in Glasgow.

The Cromford and High Peak Railway

One of the more unusual sections of British Railways was the Cromford and High Peak Railway (C&HPR). Built to connect two canals, the Cromford Canal at the south end and the Peak Forest Canal at the north, over the uplands of the Derbyshire Peak District, it opened throughout from Cromford Wharf to Whalley Bridge in 1831. The line comprised level sections with cable worked inclines between them. It was taken over by the London and North Western Railway (LNWR) in 1861 and the section north of Parsley Hay, about 14 miles from Cromford, was partially incorporated into the Buxton to Ashbourne line. Other parts of the northern section were retained as sidings or abandoned. The remaining section included three inclines, though in 1877 Hopton was converted to locomotive working, its 1 in 14 gradient being one of the steepest on BR. At the southern end the line was extended to join the Midland Railway's Derby to Manchester line at High Peak Junction. Middleton Incline closed in 1963 and the now two remaining separate sections closed in 1967. Since closure the route has been converted into a footpath.

Right: The short section of just over a mile from the top of Sheep Pasture incline to the foot of Middleton incline was worked by an engine based at Sheep Pasture Top. Latterly it was a London Midland and Scottish Kitson-built 0-4-0ST No. 47007, built in 1932, seen on shed in September 1963. The shed building had been damaged in a storm and was demolished in 1962. The LNWR signal guards the top of the incline which is behind the engine house, seen above the wagon. The steam winding engine was replaced by an electric motor in 1964. The locomotive had to be brought to site up or down the inclines.

Cromford Goods was at the bottom of Sheep Pasture incline, which is off to the left of the picture taken on 10th September 1963. Latterly both the top and bottom sections of the C&HPR were worked by ex-War Department austerity 0-6-0ST's and No.68013 is seen in the small yard near the original C&HPR buildings, while another LNWR signal guards the bottom of the incline. The line was popular with enthusiasts and a number of specials were run over it, the participants travelling in open wagons and walking the inclines. Behind the engine is the then disused and overgrown Cromford Canal, and below the canal the Midland Railway Derby to Manchester line.

Southern England and the Isle of Wight

Living in Yorkshire the Southern Region was not somewhere I was able to visit often. However, a holiday in Newquay in 1960 included a visit to Wadebridge to see the Beattie tanks and T9s. The Isle of Wight with the O2s and Hayling Island with *Terrier* tanks were a magnet and a visit was managed in December 1962. Having chased trains down the Mid Wales and Brecon & Merthyr lines we drove to Southampton. There we slept, badly, in the Mini before catching the first boat to Cowes, spending the day on the island photographing what remained of the island system, and the following day we went to Hayling Island. There followed a series of visits to the West Country with a cousin of father's kindly providing lunch near Bath. On other occasions there were visits to the Romney line as well as more trips to the Isle of Wight. A railtour to Exeter behind *Mallard* introduced me to the London and South Western Railway (LSWR) main line and some trips behind Bulleid pacifics over that superb line followed.

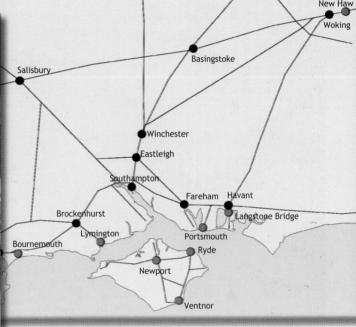

Map of Southern Locations

Above: Bournemouth Central saw ex-Great Western Railway engines in addition to the usual Southern locomotives. No.6910 *Gossington Hall* stands in the down platform with an inter-regional train which it probably took over at Oxford, its shed plate being 81F for Oxford shed. The train then proceeded to Bournemouth West where it terminated on 17th July 1963.

A week's holiday in the West Country, camping in the Landrover (not comfortable) included a visit to the Lymington branch. This was then worked by M7's; No.30480 one of the class fitted for push-pull working, has just been coaled from the wagon outside the shed at Lymington Town on 17th July 1963.

The major engineering work on the Hayling Island branch was the bridge over Langstone Harbour. *Terrier* No.32678 heads a Hayling Island train over the bridge on a sunny but cold 19th December 1962. The signal box in the centre of the bridge, which controlled the swing span, provided a convenient vantage point. After this picture we visited Basingstoke and then made the long drive back to Halifax in the dark.

Unrebuilt Bulleid *West Country* pacific No. 34002 *Salisbury* arrives at Portsmouth Harbour station on 3rd October 1965, with a Locomotive Club of Great Britain special going to the Isle of Wight for what had been planned as a farewell railtour on the Shanklin to Ventnor and the Ryde to Cowes lines, which were due to close that weekend. However, problems with bus licences caused the closures to be delayed to 21st February 1966 and 18th April 1966 respectively.

The Isle of Wight had an extensive railway system which became part of the Southern Railway in 1923. Closures in the 1950s reduced the system to the two lines from Ryde to Cowes and Ventnor. On summer Saturdays the system was very busy with holidaymakers arriving and departing by steamer at Ryde Pier Head. Traffic was heaviest on the Ventnor line with various resorts en route. Trains were all worked by former LSWR class O2s, fitted with larger bunkers. They were numbered in a separate series and named after places on the island. On 5th September 1964 the crew cleans the smokebox on W35 *Freshwater*, after arrival at Ventnor.

On the frosty morning of 21st February 1965 W17 *Seaview* was shunting at the north end of Newport yard as we ran in on the train from Cowes, hauled by W18 *Ningwood*. The remains of the Freshwater line, closed in 1953, bear right behind the engine.

Rebuilt Bulleid *West Country* pacific, No.34101 *Hartland* passes through Byfleet and New Haw on a train for Southampton on 28th July 1964. The station was West Weybridge until 1961.

The West Country

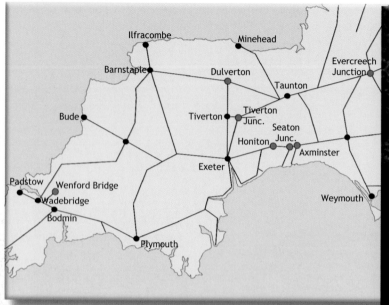

Map of West Country Locations

It was inconceivable that a visit to the West Country did not include a trip to Wenford Bridge on the Bodmin and Wadebridge. By 15th July 1963 the Beattie well tanks had been replaced by former GWR outside cylindered 0-6-0 pannier tanks. An enquiry at Wadebridge station produced tickets to travel to Wenford Bridge at a cost of six shillings. It was a damp day as can be seen in the picture taken at the watering point in Pencarrow Woods.

Left: In the early morning of 16th July 1963 we were driving to Dulverton and in a lay-by saw Devon County Council steam roller No.121, TA2438, simmering quietly. It was built by Marshalls, works no.56187, in 1911 as a traction engine for the War Department and saw service in France. After World War One it was returned to Marshalls, rebuilt as a steamroller and sold to Devon County Council. In 1967 it was preserved and has subsequently been converted back to a traction engine.

Right: Dulverton was the northern terminus of the Exe Valley line from Exeter via Tiverton and the junction with the Taunton to Barnstaple line. Most of the Exe Valley trains were auto trains worked by 14XX 0-4-2 tanks and here No.1450 takes water before the return journey to Exeter on 16th July 1963.

The branch between Tiverton Junction on the GWR main line to Exeter and Tiverton on the Exe Valley line was worked by autotrains using class 14XX 0-4-2 tanks. Here No.1442 departs from Tiverton Junction with its auto coach, whilst the up main line train is still standing in the platform on 2nd September 1964.

Later on the 2nd September No.1442 returns to Tiverton Junction with the late afternoon goods from Tiverton. The trucks will be forwarded by the main line pickup freight. No.1442 then returned light engine to Tiverton for another working with its autotrain. There were some 12 return workings daily on the 4¾ mile line.

On 3rd September 1964 unrebuilt *Battle of Britain* No. 34079 *141 Squadron* coasts down the bank from Honiton tunnel to Seaton Junction with a Plymouth to Brighton train. The gangers have not only kept the track in fine condition, but have time to grow vegetables beside the line.

Further down Honiton bank rebuilt *Battle of Britain* No 34052 *Lord Dowding* drifts down to Seaton Junction with a mixed freight, including some wagons of ballast which may well have come from Meldon Quarry, on 3rd September 1964.

Axminster, further east on the Southern main line from London to Exeter, was the junction for the Lyme Regis branch. Class S15 4-6-0 No.30832 heads an all stations train to Exeter whilst the postman waits on the up platform for a London bound train on 16th July 1963.

The Somerset and Dorset Joint line was a delightful cross country route with some splendid bucolic names. One such was Evercreech Junction where the Highbridge branch left the main line to Bath. Closure came on 6th April 1966 and on the previous Friday the last school train from Highbridge leaves Evercreech Junction for Templecombe, headed by 2-6-2T No.41249.

Welsh Narrow Gauge in the 1960s

My introduction to the Talyllyn Railway at Easter 1959 quickly led to visits to the other lines then operating. The Ffestiniog Railway (FR) ran from Porthmadog to Tan-y-Bwlch and the Vale of Rheidol ran from Aberystwyth to Devil's Bridge. These were both visited in 1959, the trip from Tywyn to the FR being via Bala and a walk from Maentwrog Road station to Tan-y-Bwlch. The station nameboard at Maentwrog proclaimed 'Tan-y-Bwlch 3 Miles', but I had failed to realise that it was firstly down a long hill to the Oakley Arms and then a steep climb to Tan-y-Bwlch station, and I only just caught the train. The quarry lines at Penrhyn and Dinorwic were still working and a little later the Welshpool re-opened.

These lines, as well as the others which have closed, have been of interest over the decades and most of the lifted lines walked. However, some of the closed lines have been rebuilt and re-opened. For example, walking through the Pass of Aberglaslyn on the trackbed of the former Welsh Highland Railway (WHR) in 1961, it was inconceivable that, nearly 50 years later, it would be possible to have the same experience travelling in a genuine WHR coach.

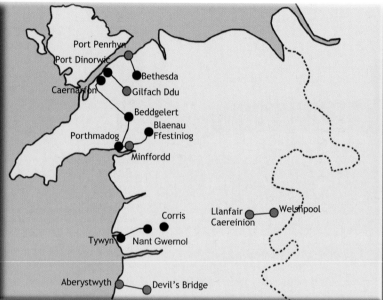

Map of Locations

Left: The Vale of Rheidol Railway, which opened in 1902 from Aberystwyth to Devil's Bridge, has always been mainly a tourist line. In 1923 the Great Western Railway acquired the line and in the interwar period re-equipped it with a standardised fleet of three 2-6-2 tanks and coaches designed for the tourist traffic. With the closure of the Welshpool line it became British Railways' last narrow gauge line and went on to become the last steam-worked part of the national system, the locomotives being the only ones to carry the BR blue livery. In 1964 the coaches, which had been in GWR chocolate and cream, were painted green and lettered 'VR', though the locomotives were still in lined BR green. Here No.9 *Prince of Wales* climbs the 1 in 50 gradient out of Aberffrwd towards Devil's Bridge on 30th May 1964.

The Dinorwic quarries at Llanberis had a large internal system using 1 ft 10¾ in gauge, and made use of inclines to bring slate wagons down to Gilfach Ddu at Llanberis. Here the Padarn Railway ran to Port Dinorwic, about seven miles away. It was 4 ft gauge and the slate wagons were carried on transporters between Gilfach Ddu and the top of the incline down to the port. Originally worked by two 0-4-0 tender engines built in 1848, one of which, *Fire Queen*, is preserved, the line was later equipped with three 0-6-0 tanks built by Hunslet. Here on a wet July day in 1961, shortly before the line closed, *Amalthaea*, built in 1886, waits at Gilfach Ddu with the train to the coast.

The Penrhyn quarry line from the quarry at Bethesda to Port Penrhyn near Bangor was built to the quarry gauge of 1 ft 10¾ in. Its main line was worked by three large Hunslet 0-4-0 saddle tanks. Here one of them, *Blanche*, stands outside the shed at Port Penrhyn, before working to the quarry. In the background a BR 2-6-0 is working the branch from the North Wales coast line to the port to collect any slate and to deliver coal for the quarry lines. The Penrhyn Quarry main line closed in 1962, but the three engines survived. *Blanche* and *Linda* went to the Ffestiniog Railway where they were rebuilt as 2-4-0 saddle tanks and are still at work, while *Charles* is preserved at the nearby Penrhyn Castle.

The section of the Welshpool and Llanfair Light Railway east of Llanfair runs along the banks of the River Banwy. Locomotive No.1 *The Earl* heads a train of Upnor carriages past the remains of the weir, which formerly served Dolrhyd Mill, with a train for Heniarth a journey of about 1¼ miles in April 1965. Floods the previous December had severely damaged one of the piers of the Banwy bridge, just east of Heniarth. Assistance from the 16th Railway Regiment Royal Engineers repaired the bridge and trains resumed to Castle Caereinion on 14th August 1965.

Ffestiniog trains passing at Minffordd on 15th July 1964. *Prince*, one of the original engines built by George England in 1863 and much rebuilt, is heading a down train. The former Penrhyn locomotive *Blanche* is heading the train to Tan-y-Bwlch. On the Ffestiniog trains use the right hand track at loops.

Isle of Man

The Isle of Man with its system of 3 ft gauge steam railways, as well as the 3 ft gauge Manx Electric Railway (MER) and the 3 ft 6 ins gauge Snaefell Mountain Railway (SMR), plus the Douglas horse trams, became something of a transport museum. In the 1950s the MER found itself unable to continue and was taken over by the government. At the end of 1965 the Isle of Man Railway, which also ran the bus services outside Douglas, decided to close the railway operation. For a year nothing ran and the end of the last common carrier narrow gauge railway in the British Isles seemed certain. However, in spring 1967 the Marquis of Ailsa leased the system and re-opened all the three lines to Peel, Ramsey and Castletown. The line from Castletown to Port Erin reopened in 1968. There were operating losses and the Marquis closed the Peel and Ramsey lines at the end of the 1968 season. Trains continued to run to Port Erin with a government subsidy and when the Marquis withdrew at the end of the 1971 season the old company took over running the railway with the subsidy. After a period when the future looked uncertain the Manx government bought the railway and buses and, though there have been ups and downs, both the steam and electric railways are now in good shape.

Railways of the Isle of Man

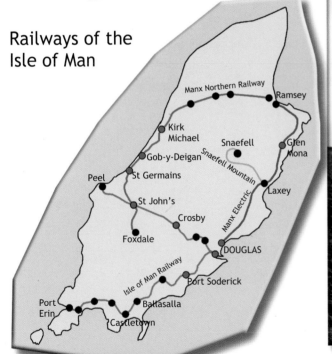

Above: The two principal engineering works were the viaducts at Glen Wyllin and Glen Mooar on the Ramsey line south of Kirk Michael. Both were rebuilt after the First World War, with Glen Wyllin having plate girders whilst Glen Mooar retained lattice girders. No.8 *Fenella* heads north over Glen Mooar viaduct with the morning Douglas to Ramsey train in July 1964.

The Marquis of Ailsa reopened the railway on 3rd June 1967 with a special train and services from Douglas to Peel. On the following day the Ramsey line reopened and services ran to Castletown on 11th June 1967. The laying of a gas pipe along the lineside delayed opening to Port Erin until 11th July 1968. At this time the locomotives were all repainted in light green, now known as Ailsa green, and here the last of the opening day trains, headed by No.8 *Fenella*, is seen at Greeba between Crosby and St Johns. The discs on the engine were an innovation of Sir Philip Wombwell, Bt, who was Ailsa's manager in 1967.

An intensive service was operated in 1967, requiring all five workable locomotives and the ex-County Donegal railcars. Here trains pass at Port Soderick, with No.12 *Hutchinson* waiting with a Castletown to Douglas train, whilst No.5 *Mona* arrives from Douglas with a train for Castletown in the summer of that year.

Probably the scenic highlight of the Isle of Man Railway was the section at Gob-y-Deigan, between St Germains and Kirk Michael where the Ramsey line ran above the sea. However, the terrain was unstable and regular maintenance was needed. Here No.11 *Maitland* heads a Ramsey to Douglas train in summer 1968, the last year trains ran to Ramsey. The track bed is now a footpath.

Derby Castle, at the northern end of Douglas promenade, is the terminus of the Horse Tramway and the interchange point with the Manx Electric Railway. The horse trams are now only a shadow of their former glory, but in July 1964 it was busy. A tram is leaving for the sea terminal, two miles away at the south end of the promenade, while several trams wait to enter the tram terminus under the overall roof. The conductor has probably already collected the fares of the two passengers. A Douglas Corporation bus on the promenade route pulls out of the depot area and a Manx Electric train waits to depart for Laxey. On the right is the road sweeper which ran regularly up and down the tram tracks clearing up behind the horses, for obvious reasons!

The Edwardian style of the Manx Electric Railway (MER) publicity continued into the 1970s, and described the journey as 'a continuous panorama of mountain, glen and marine scenery'. This is illustrated by a Ramsey-bound train at Glen Mona, between Laxey and Ramsey in July 1964. The power car is one of the winter saloons, which have provided the backbone of the regular service since 1899, though, as it is a warm day the open trailer is clearly more popular. On the station the post box by the shelter was one of a number on the MER which were emptied by the conductors, who were sworn in as auxiliary postmen.

Douglas station was impressive, with two island platforms, a glassed concourse as well as the main shed and works. The southern platform was used by Port Erin trains and the northern one by Peel and Ramsey trains. In the summer of 1964 there were two heavy trains with about eight coaches leaving Douglas at 10 am and 10.30 am for Port Erin to cater for day trippers to the various places in the south of the Island. The comparable return workings reached Douglas in the late afternoon to give visitors time to get to their hotels and boarding houses for high tea. These trains needed banking assistance over the heavy gradients north of Ballasalla and the afternoon Douglas to Port Erin train was double-headed as far as Ballasalla to provide the banker. Here No.1 *Sutherland* pilots No.11 *Maitland* out of Douglas. No.1 was already working on reduced boiler pressure and would be withdrawn at the end of the season.

At the end of the day at Douglas as the engines return to the shed. From left to right they are No.8 *Fenella*, No.1 *Sutherland*, No.12 *Hutchinson* & No.5 *Mona*. Douglas and the east end of St John's were the only signalled installations on the railway. The signals seen here in July 1964 are for the engine release road between the island platforms and the inner face of the north island platform.

Industrial Scenes

Bradford Corporation operated a large sewage works east of the city at Esholt in the Aire valley. Here there was a standard gauge railway system which connected with the Leeds to Skipton line just north of Apperley Bridge. The last locomotive bought for the works was *Elizabeth*, built in 1958 by Hudswell Clarke and designed to burn the grease extracted at the sewage works, which came from the wool being washed in the many mills in the city. It is seen outside the loco shed on 25th July 1963. *Elizabeth* is now preserved at Armley Mills Industrial Museum in Leeds.

The 2 ft 6 in gauge railway linking Bowaters' paper mills at Sittingbourne and Kelmsley with the dock at Ridham was one of the last industrial, as opposed to mining, railways to use steam. It operated around the clock and there was an internal passenger service for staff. At Sittingbourne mill in April 1966 0-6-2T *Superb*, built by Bagnall in 1922, shunts some passenger stock amidst the industrial background of the works. The location, on the Thames Estuary, was exposed to winter winds hence the sliding panel which can protect the cab. After closure in 1969 the southern part of the line was passed to the Sittingbourne and Kelmsley Light Railway, which operates as a tourist attraction. *Superb* is based on the line today.

Two of the 0-6-2T's stand at Kelmsley Mill in April 1966, *Triumph*, built by Bagnall in 1934, which also operates on the Sittingbourne and Kelmsley Light Railway, while behind is *Superb*. The railway was very well maintained and at closure some of the locomotives and stock went on to form the nucleus of the Whipsnade Zoo Railway.

Below: George Cohen (Machinery) Ltd, part of 600 Group, had a depot on Town Street, Stanningley, near Leeds. It had a rail connection to the former GNR Leeds to Bradford line. Cohen's system crossed Town Street which had formerly had the tracks of Leeds City Tramways laid along it. There were at least two locomotives at the works, an 0-4-0ST built by Kitson, and an 0-6-0ST Hunslet, works no.1705, delivered to Sir Lindsay Parkinson & Co. Ltd in 1937 for their works at the Royal Ordnance Factory, Chorley. It is seen here propelling a wagon across Town Street into the works on the south side on 16th October 1963. The number 600 on the engine refers to the company and is not an engine number. It was scrapped in June 1965.

Above: Huddersfield gas works, latterly part of North Eastern Gas Board, was served by a branch from the former MR Huddersfield branch terminus at Newtown. Opened in 1910 the line was part of a grandiose scheme of expansion in the West Riding, but it never had a passenger service. The line to the gasworks passed under the viaduct carrying the main line into the town and then along Beaumont Street to enter the works across Leeds Road and the canal. Opened in 1922 and closed in 1966, it was worked by two 0-4-0ST's built by Peckett. Here one of the locomotives runs up Beaumont Street towards Newtown Yard with the gas works in the background in 1960.

Austria

My first overseas railway trip was to Austria in summer 1966, when a friend and I drove there in my Mini. Austria still had a large number of steam-worked narrow gauge lines and plenty of standard gauge steam, not to mention the scenery. Several other visits were made, including one the following year when we also went to Czechoslovakia.

Map of Locations

One of the most unusual lines was the Erzbergbahn (Iron Mountain railway), a standard gauge rack railway. This ran from Eisenerz in the north, where it connected with the branch to Hieflau on the Amstetten to Selzthal line, to Vordernberg. Here it connected with a branch to Leoben on the Vienna to Klagenfurt main line. Ore was worked south over the summit at Prabichl from the mine south of Eisenerz and also worked out north to Hieflau. The line was worked by a fleet of rack/adhesion engines. Class 97 were 0-6-2T locomotives introduced in 1890 and class 197 0-12-0T's introduced in 1912. Two class 297 2-12-2T's were introduced in 1941, but were reported to damage the track. These were out of use when I visited, and stored away from the line. Most freight trains were topped and tailed, and often double-headed as well. Here a train of empties climbs between Vordernberg and Prabichl, the summit of the line, with two class 97s.

Class 197 No.302, an 0-12-0T, propels a rake of hoppers out of Eisenerz up to the mines. It will shortly get onto the rack section. The class 197's were built in 1912 and designed by Karl Golsdorf, the mechanical engineer of the State Railway from 1893 to 1916.

Empty hoppers being worked up the branch from Hieflau to Eisenerz in May 1967, where the train will be taken over by one of the class 197 0-12-0T rack and adhesion engines and propelled to the mine. The locomotive is class 50, No.50-1022, 2-10-0. A German Railways design, which were built in various countries during the war. After the conflict many locomotives were retained in former occupied countries including Austria.

760 mm gauge, (2 ft 6 in) was used for most narrow gauge railways throughout the former Austro-Hungarian Empire. In Austria there are some 16 narrow gauge lines, several of considerable length. Many were operated by the Austrian Federal Railways (OBB) but in the south eastern province of Styria a number of lines were operated by the provincial government, the Steiermarkische Landesbahnen (StLB). The Murtalbahn ran from Unzmarkt to Mauterndorf, a distance of 76 km, and was opened in 1894. Headed by a classic Austrian 0-6-2T the afternoon train from Unzmarkt to Mauterndorf leaves Stadl-Kaltwasser, west of Murau, where it has crossed an Unzmarkt-bound mixed train in July 1966. U.43 was built by Krauss-Linz in 1913.

The Postlingbergbahn is a tramway up the Postlingberg, a hill about 250 m high from which there are panoramic views of Linz, a city on the Danube west of Vienna. Opened in 1898 the metre gauge tramway connected with the city tramway at Urfahr, and has gradients steeper than 1 in 10. Through running was originally not possible as the Linz trams are 900 mm gauge and Postlingberhbahn used a form of caliper brake necessitating the special pointwork shown. Unusually the cars were numbered with Roman numerals. In 2008 the line was rebuilt to 900 mm gauge to allow through running. New cars were built but several of the older cars were regauged and re-equipped, including VIII which is seen here at the summit station in July 1966.

The Steiermarkische Landesbahnen (StLB) line from Wiez to Ratten is a narrow gauge extension of a standard gauge StLB branch from Gleisdorf, near Graz. Opened from Weiz to Birkfeld (24 km) in 1911. Later in 1930 the line was extended further up the Feistritz valley to Ratten (42 km). At the time of my visit in July 1966 there was only one train a day to and from Ratten, the others terminating at Birkfeld. Here 0-6-2T No.U8 heads a Birkfeld train over the viaduct near Hart-Puch. My blue Mini, in which we had travelled to Austria stands on the roadside, together with Neil Chapman who accompanied me on the visit.

St Polten, a major junction on the Vienna to Linz main line, had a small tramway system, hidden away behind the railway station, which ran 9.4 km to Harland. Opened in 1911 it also conveyed goods wagons to factories along the route. Passengers were carried in a small fleet of four wheeled tramcars. The original cars of 1911, built by Grazer Waggonfabrik, survived until closure in 1976. In the picture car No.1 heads towards Harland along the single track in July 1966. There were also a couple of four wheeled electric locomotives for the freight traffic. Much of the rolling stock has been preserved, a reminder of a classic small central European tramway system.

A short standard gauge branch ran from Murzzuschlag, at the western end of the Semmering Pass, to Neuberg. The branch was worked by the last surviving class 91 2-6-0 tanks. Designed by Karl Golsdorf they were introduced in 1908 and were an update of an earlier 1898 design with larger water capacity. Here 91.107 stands at Neuberg with its train of three four-wheeled coaches waiting to depart for Murzzuschlag in July 1966. We were able to enjoy a footplate ride on the vintage locomotive. Sadly the class became extinct in 1972.

On the 1967 visit to Austria we also visited Czechoslovakia. We did get arrested but having visas which stated 'purpose of visit - railway photography', resolved that difficulty and we obtained a letter, which of course we could not read, stating we had permission to photograph. The class 475 4-8-2 was built by Skoda between 1947 and 1950 and was a mixed traffic engine. This design formed the basis for all subsequent new steam locomotives, and two of the class have been preserved. Unfortunately my notes do not record the location but it is somewhere north east of Bratislava in May 1967.

Portugal

In the 1960s Portugal was a still a dictatorship under Salazar and was relatively undeveloped. I cannot recall exactly why Gavin Morrison and I decided to go, but we must have seen pictures of the superbly maintained though rather elderly locomotives on both the 5 ft 6 in gauge and the extensive metre gauge systems. We flew to Lisbon and then headed north to Oporto which was the centre of much of the steam operation. We hired a Mini on an unlimited mileage basis and I recall the rather shocked reaction on returning it a few days later at Lisbon Airport when they saw the mileage we had done. The sun shone and we saw a fascinating variety of locomotives. The metre gauge 0-4-4-0T compound Mallets on the Oporto systems were probably my favourite; very much a gentleman's sporting locomotive with a racy appearance.

Location Map

Left: Sao Bento, the broad gauge terminal station in Oporto, was a very period place with a high overall roof and the platforms going almost to the tunnel mouth. From here the lines rose to connect with the main north-south line at Campanha. It was also highly decorated with tiles, a feature of many Portuguese stations. No.238, a Borsig-built four-cylinder compound of 1904 stands in the station on 8th September 1967. It was owned originally by the Minho Douro Railway, which had constructed the lines from Oporto to the north and east, and became part of the state owned system in 1947. Happily No.238 has been preserved. The chimney mounted numberplates were a feature of Portuguese locomotives.

An afternoon Oporto to Peso de Régua train in the Douro Valley, just west of Peso de Régua at Caldas de Moledo on 9th September 1967. The train of four wheeled carriages is headed by 2-6-4T No.088, built in 1920 by the Swiss Locomotive and Machine works (SLM).

There was an extensive network of metre gauge lines around Oporto, with four other lines branching off the Douro valley line to the east of Oporto serving various valleys. Further south the Vouga lines connected two stations on the Lisbon to Oporto line, Aveiro and Espinho, serving a hilly area to the east. At Sernada do Vouga, the operational centre, a line headed east to Viseu where it joined another line heading south to St Comba Dao to connect with a broad gauge line. Vouzela was in the middle of the 70km Sernada to Viseu section. In the picture a Viseu to Sernada train headed by No.E131 passes a Viseu-bound train hauled by Borsig 4-6-0T No.E122 on 10th September 1967. E131 is a 2-8-2T built by Henschel in 1924 and is piloting one of the Borsig 4-6-0T's of 1908, No.E121. The station building is covered in a magnificent bougainvillea.

The Viseu to Sernada train crosses one of the many viaducts on that line, with Nos.E131 and E121 in charge on 10th September 1967.

No.283, an inside cylindered 4-6-0 built by Henschel in 1910, accelerates away from Oporto, Campanha station, with a train of modern coaches bound for the Douro Valley line on 12th September 1967. Most of the broad gauge engines had been converted to oil firing, Portugal having no coal deposits.

The metre gauge network north of Oporto started at Trindade station in the city centre, opened in the mid 1930s when the line was extended from Boa Vista, and double track installed between Trindade and Senhora da Hora. There was a commuter service as well as the longer distance trains, and the line is now part of the Oporto metro. No.E167 is a 0-4-4-0 compound Mallet bult by Henschel in 1908. Originally on the various Douro Valley lines they were latterly concentrated on the Oporto lines, and No.E167 is seen at Trindade awaiting departure on 8th September 1967.

East Africa

From its formation in 1948 when the Kenya Uganda Railway and the Tanganyika Railway were merged, East African Railways (EAR) operated an efficient metre gauge system, together with associated lake and road services. One of the major users of Garratt type locomotives, its fleet of maroon engines was well maintained. Lack of indigenous coal resulted in the oil firing. Whilst much of the traffic was freight, there were excellent long distance passenger trains with dining and sleeping carriages.

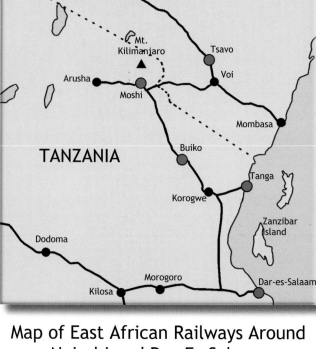

Map of East African Railways Around Nairobi and Dar-Es-Salaam

In 1963 the line linking the Tanzanian Central line and the Tanga line was opened allowing through service between Dar-es-Salaam and Nairobi. The twice weekly train took 47 hours for the 650 mile journey and the train conveyed a variety of through carriages. Here is the train in 1970, having left Dar-es-Salaam at 9 am, it is approaching the marshalling yards at Ilala on the outskirts of the city. Headed by No.6019, a 4-8-2+2-8-4 class 60 Garratt, a regular performer in the early 1970s, which will take the train to Moshi arriving at 8 am the following morning, the train has coaches and a buffet car for Nairobi as well as through coaches for Tanga. These will be detached at Korogwe.

Nairobi shed, the largest shed on the EAR, was home to the class 59 Garratts built by Beyer Peacock in 1955, as well as a wide range of other locomotives. By 1976 it was becoming rather dilapidated. Here we see the bunkers of No.5913 *Mount Debasien*, and No.5909 *Mount Mgahinga*, already turned for their next trips to Mombasa. No.3020 *Nyaturu*, a 2-8-4 with a twelve wheeled tender, was really a Tanzanian engine the class 30s being designed for the Central Line and built by North British in 1955/6. The class 30 had come to Nairobi for overhaul and when the border closed it had to remain in Kenya. Happily it has been preserved and currently works the occasional special out of Nairobi.

After overhaul locomotives were sent out on trial double-heading a service train. Here light Garratt No.6018 pilots No.5510 on a freight off the Thika line at Makadara, just east of Nairobi on 28th August 1976. The class 60's were built by Franco-Belge (6001-6012) in 1953 and Beyer Peacock (6013-6029) in 1954, while the class 55's were built by Beyer Peacock in 1945. No.5510 was originally supplied to the Burma Railways and bought by EAR in 1952.

West of Nairobi the line to Uganda climbs through fertile farm land to the summit at Uplands before descending into the Rift Valley. No.2930 *Tiriki*, a class 29 built by North British in 1955, drifts into Muguga in September 1976 with a Nairobi bound pickup goods.

The line from Tanga, on the northern Tanzanian coast, to Moshi, at the foot of Mount Kilimanjaro, was built as the *NordBahn* by the German colonial government reaching Moshi in 1914. Here No.2917 *Kisii* enters Buiko with the Tanga to Moshi pickup train in 1970.

In 1976 all through freight trains between Mombasa and Nairobi were hauled by 4-8-2 + 2-8-4 class 59 Garratts. Introduced in 1955 and weighing 252 tons they were the largest steam engines then working anywhere in the world. They were restricted to the Mombasa to Nairobi line and could take up to 1,200 tons, the journey taking about 21 hours for the 332 miles. Trains were caboose worked. Two sets of crews were carried, one working the train and the other resting in the caboose. There were two crew changes at specified stations. Here on 5th September 1976 No.5918 *Mount Gelai* has just left Tsavo and is climbing across the arid Tsavo plains. The building of the bridge over the Tsavo river in 1898 was seriously delayed by the activities of two lions, known as the 'man-eaters of Tsavo', who were reputedly responsible for the deaths of over one hundred construction workers, before finally being shot. No.5918 has been preserved and has worked several charter trains on the Nairobi to Mombasa line. It is currently in need of some repairs but is basically in working order.

The link line from the Central line of Tanzania joined the Tanga to Moshi line at Mruazi, 40 miles from Tanga. Exchange of traffic from Tanga to Dar-es-Salaam took place at Korogwe 12 miles further on. The train connecting into the Dar to Nairobi train left Tanga at 4.30 pm and conveyed through coaches to Moshi and Mombasa. Normally worked by a class 29 2-8-4, a class 24 4-8-0 was put on by special request. A letter to the shedmaster at Tanga instructed that it be cleaned to 'ultimate resplendentness'. As the line was paralleled by the road for the first five miles out of Tanga EAR kindly provided a car so I could photograph it before riding the rest of the journey to Korogwe. No.2415 is seen about a mile out of Tanga, with exhaust as requested. The class 24's were built for the Kenya Uganda Railway by Vulcan Foundry and Nasmyth Wilson between 1922 and 1930. No.2415 was built in 1923.

The Moshi to Dar-es-Salaam traffic was all Garratt worked in 1970 and here No.6011 awaits departure with a Dar-es-Salaam bound freight in Moshi station with the snow-capped peak of Kilimanjaro in the background.

Angola and Nigeria

Working in Nigeria on several occasions gave the opportunity to see something of Nigerian Railways, though photography during the civil war was difficult. A developing interest in African railways led to the desire to see the railways in Angola, especially the Benguela Railway with its wood burning Garratts. The chance for this came in 1973 when I was able to return home from a year in Zambia via Luanda. Angola was then a Portuguese colony and communication with Zambia was non-existent, so the arrangements had to be made via my mother in Halifax.

In Angola there were four separate railway systems all running inland from the coast. Two state operated systems were the Luanda lines in the north, and the Mocamedes lines in the south. South of the Luanda line was the 60 cm gauge Amboim Railway, and between that and the Mocamedes, the Benguela Railway, which provided a through route to the Congo passing on into Zambia and Rhodesia. A couple of years after my visit the Portuguese withdrew and in the ensuing civil war the railways were destroyed. They are now being rebuilt with Chinese aid. However, there will no longer be the immaculate Garratts, but the all-conquering diesels operating the line.

The Luanda Railway's (CFA) inspection trolley, CFL ZA 21, on the 60 cm line from Canhoca to Golungo Alto in Angola on 11th May 1973. It had been sent up the line after the afternoon train to Golungo Alto to return me to Canhoca as there was no suitable return train, and no suitable accommodation in Golungo. It is posed on a bridge about 5 km from Canhoca. I did not fancy walking on the bridge so the trolley dropped me on terra firma and reversed back on to the bridge for the photograph. The driver is standing on the bridge and Inspector Robeiro, who accompanied me on the CFA is sitting in the trolley. Not only did he arrange all the travel and trains, but also visits to the Braganca Falls near Malange and the botanical gardens at Salazar.

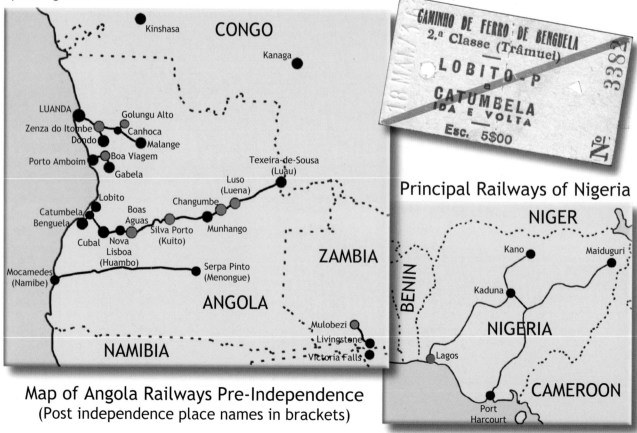

Map of Angola Railways Pre-Independence
(Post independence place names in brackets)

Principal Railways of Nigeria

The 3 ft 6 ins gauge Luanda system had a main line to Malange, with two branches, one off to the south to Dondo and a 60cm gauge line to Golungu Alto. This latter system was worked by three 0-8-2T locomotives built by Orenstein and Koppel. One, No.65, was in the works in Luanda being converted to oil firing. The other two, Nos.61 & 63 were at Canhoca and burned wood. Here is No.63 having arrived at Golungu on 11th May 1873 with the combined guards van and fuel truck behind the engine.

The junction for the Dondo branch was Zenza, and the branch trains were the only regular steam workings on the 3 ft 6 in lines of the Luanda system. They were worked by Henschel built 4-8-0s dating from 1923. No.156 has typical Portuguese chimney number plates and has been converted to oil burning. Like most of the CFA stock it was converted from metre gauge to 3 ft 6 in in 1963 when the linking of the various systems in Angola was proposed, which would connect with the rest of the southern African systems via the Benguela Railway. General Motors diesel No.109 heads the Luanda to Malange train on 14th May 1973.

The 123 km, 60 cm gauge, Amboim Railway had opened in the mid 1920s to link the coffee growing areas around Gabela, on the plateau, with Porto Amboim on the coast. Robert Hudson of Leeds had provided much of the equipment. In 1973 the service was very sparse with a weekly mixed train in each direction, taking about 12 hours, and two return trips of a Wickham railcar. When planning the trip the management were most helpful, but insisted the mixed was slow and much less comfortable than the railcar. We compromised by travelling one day from Gabela on the railcar, which took about 5 hours, and then travelling on the mixed the following morning. I was the sole occupant of the first class carriage and at each of the many stops the guard appeared with a tray bearing a bottle of cold beer and a glass! The first 80 km were fairly level but from Boa Viagem the line climbed steeply up the escarpment to Gabela. At Boa Viagem on 16th May 1973 the locomotive, No.61, a 2-8-0T Henschel of 1950, exchanged tenders so it had a full load of wood for the climb. The train is in the distance and behind is the escarpment. Sadly the line is thought to have closed about 1975.

The Benguela Railway (CFB) was the largest system in Angola. Its line extended 1347 km from the port of Lobito to Texeira-de-Sousa (Luau) on the Congo border where it connected with the Bas Congo Katanga railway to provide a direct outlet for the Congolese and Zambian minerals to the sea. Until the civil war it was largely steam worked though some General Electric diesels were introduced for working the Cubal Variant, opened in 1974 to shorten and ease the route between Benguela on the coast and Cubal on the plateau. The majority of the locomotives burned wood, though some coal was used on the coastal section, and there were oil fired Garratts used on the Benguela to Cubal section which was arid. The CFB had large plantations of eucalyptus to provide fuel. Class 9C, No.229, a 4-8-0 built by North British in 1929 stands by the fuelling stages at Boas Aguas, 46 km east of Nova Lisboa (Huambo) with the twice weekly Lobito to Texeira-de-Sousa passenger train on 19th May 1973.

Locomotive No.229, a class 9C 4-8-0, has taken over the west-bound passenger train at Silva Porto (Kuito) on 22nd May 1973, and its tender is piled high with wood. CFB passenger stock was classic southern African wooden bodied carriages with a clerestory roof and open balconies mainly dating from the late 1920s. The two high roofed coaches were built in the 1960s for Rhodesia Railways by Metro Cammell, but not delivered because of the introduction of sanctions and then sold to the CFB.

Because of the risk of attack the passenger trains east of Silva Porto (Kuito) had an armoured speeder run in front and in radio contact with the train engine. Class 9C No.231, built by North British in 1929, has armour plating round the cab and the driver carried a machine gun. There were also armed soldiers on the coaches. This is the westbound train at Changumbe on 21st May 1973, one of the fuelling points between Luso (Luena) and Munhango. The train will spend the night at Munhango where the station and yards were fortified.

Luso (Luena), 1032 km from Lobito, was the last intermediate depot before Texiera (Luau). Trains would all change engines here, and at the time of my visit trains only ran in daylight because of possible attacks by freedom fighters. In the cool of the early morning class 10B No.322, a 4-8-2+2-8-4 Garrett build by Beyer Peacock in 1929, heads a westbound train out of the yard on 21st May 1973. In order to work the volume of traffic trains ran 'Dupla' with a second engine and train coupled behind the first. The second engine can be seen in the distance.

Nigeria Railways operated an extensive 3 ft 6 in gauge system with lines running from the coast at Lagos and Port Harcourt heading north to join at Kaduna, with extensions further north to Kano and east to Maiduguri. River class No.176 2-8-2 *River Ajali*, constructed by North British in 1951, leaves Apapa Docks in Lagos in August 1969 with a transfer freight to Ebute Metta Junction, which was the site of the main marshalling yard in the Lagos area, as well as the sheds and works. The River class was introduced in 1948 with further batches being supplied up to 1954. It served as the prototype for the East African Railways class 29's and the Malawi Railways G class.

Last Train to Mulobezi

The Zambezi Sawmills Railway (ZSR) was an industrial line running northwest from Livingstone, on the north bank of the Zambezi near Victoria Falls, to the sawmills at Mulobezi, (see page 126) some 120 miles away. In addition there were many miles of semi-permanent tracks from Mulobezi into the forest areas. It was famous for its collection of ex-Rhodesia Railways (RR) and South African Railways (SAR) locos, many of which lay around the shed at Livingstone in various states of dereliction.

This line was immortalised by David Shepherd in his film *Last Train to Mulobezi*,

actually filmed shortly after the line had passed to Zambia Railways (ZR). Opened in stages from about 1926, it closed on 31st January 1973 following the closure of the sawmills, but the passenger service was taken over by ZR the following week. The sheds at Livingstone are a museum with many of the old locomotives on display.

Riding on the balcony on the last coach at night, with the stars brilliant in the African sky and the showers of sparks from the wood-burning locomotive, was an unforgettable experience.

Right: Working on the Copper Belt in the north of Zambia in 1972 made a trip to Livingstone to see the ZSR essential. A visit in November enabled me to visit the sheds and station at Livingstone, and to follow the train leaving for the overnight journey as far as Simonga, about 9 miles away. This was where the line left the Zambezi Valley and the road to head northwards. The ZSR did not renumber the engines it bought and here ex-Malawi Railways G class 2-8-2 No.57 heads the train away from the water tank at Simonga on 18th November 1972. No.57 had been built by North British in 1957 and purchased by the ZSR in February 1970. It was similar to the East African Railways 29 class and the Nigerian Railways River class. Like all the engines it burned wood.

Following the November 1972 visit I contacted the ZSR about travelling over the line. "It would be no problem", they said, "just let us know when". However at the end of January 1973 I received a call saying the last northbound train would be Friday 30th January. Just time for a quick flight to Livingstone and the purchase of food and drink, along with a torch, before catching the train, travelling in the ex-RR 1st/2nd coach. The train was hauled by No.57. The following morning Graham Roberts, who ran the railway, met me off the train and provided an excellent breakfast. Several other engines were in steam and at the shed ex-RR 10th class 4-8-2 No.156 was being prepared for the final run back to Livingstone that night. In this view of Mulobezi sheds on 31st January 1973, No.156, built by North British in 1922 and brought by the ZSR in 1960, is in the shed, while No.955 is by the water tank. No.955 is a SAR 7th class, built by Neilson in 1892 and purchased by the ZSR in 1966.

Ex-RR 10th Class, No.156 (though with the tender off No.154) is fuelled outside Mulobezi shed in preparation for the last ZSR train to Livingstone on 31st January 1973. On the left the connecting bus from Kaoma brings passengers for the train. There is no satisfactory road between Mulobezi and Livingstone, and for that reason the Zambia Railways (ZR) took over the running of the line the following week. The Sawmills company had been taken over by the Government through its investment company INDECO in 1972. The first ZR train used RR (now ZR) 12th class, No.193 and the ZSR stock and ran north on 3rd February. A week later ZR stock was in use. Latest reports suggest a weekly diesel hauled train still runs and there have been specials over the line in recent years using No.156. Thunder clouds can be seen building in the background.

It was a dull damp dawn when No.156 completed the last trip from Mulobezi. The departure from Mulobezi on 31st January 1973 was made in a thunder storm, which, together with the detonators on the track, gave it a Wagnerian feel. There were eight of us on the footplate for the first part of the journey. Nos.156 and 993, a SAR 7th class 4-8-0 and the composite coach, ex-RR 1808, were presented to David Shepherd by President Kaunda. No.993 and the coach came to UK and after being in various locations are now at the NRM and should be on display at Shildon. No.156 remained in Africa and has subsequently been restored to working order and used on specials over the line. The metal headboard had been welded on the previous day and remained on the locomotive for many years.

Southern Africa

In September 1968 the RCTS and Ian Allan ran a three-week railtour to South Africa, one of the first tours to that part of the world. The contrast with the last days of BR steam was huge. The lines we covered varied from the Transkaroo main line, double track and an endless procession of heavy freight trains hauled by huge and generally immaculate locomotives, to the Cape Town to Port Elizabeth line, single and heavily graded with Garratts toiling up the Montegue Pass.

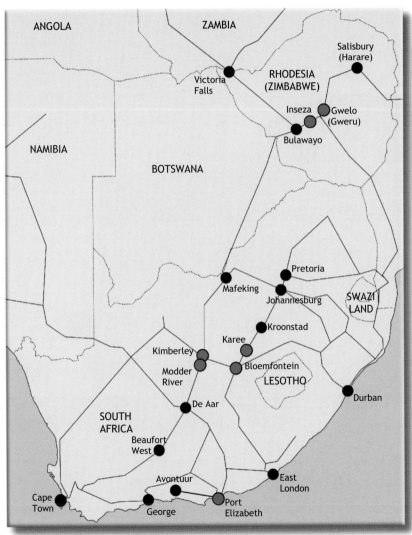

Map of Southern Africa Locations

The long distance SAR trains all had dining cars. These were either double or single diners. Double diners had separate vehicles for the kitchen and staff facilities and the dining saloon, which would seat about 48 people. Single diners had the kitchen and dining saloon in one vehicle and seated about 24. The RCTS party travelled from Cape Town to Port Elizabeth in October 1968, a journey of about 36 hours with two nights on the train. Due to the gradients, which included about 17 miles of 1 in 35 up the Montegue pass, the train weight was restricted and there was only a single diner, No.183 *Kumani*, dated from the 1920s. Here some of the party have afternoon tea. Seated on the left is the well known photographer, 'Cam' Camwell.

SAR had several 2 ft gauge lines, the longest of which was the Port Elizabeth to Avontuur line. Its main traffic was fruit to the docks at the port. Whilst the main line was worked by class NG15 2-8-2s and class NGG 13 & 16 2-6-2 + 2-6-2 Garratts, the shunting in the dock area, which had both 2 ft and 3 ft 6 in tracks, was done by the remaining class NGG 11 2-6-0 + 0-6-2 engines. In October 1968 No.54, built in 1925, shunts a chilled van towards the storage sheds where the fruit will be kept until it is put on board ship.

The Kimberley to De Aar line was very heavily trafficked and was double tracked. Here a southbound coal train approaches Modder River, south of Kimberley on 5th May 1973. It is double-headed by two class 25NC 4-8-4s, the leading one, No.3405 unofficially named *Ester*. The 25NC's were built in 1953, a non-condensing version of the class 25 introduced in 1951. All up they weighed 223 tons and had a tractive effort of 45,360 lb, impressive machines on 3 ft 6 in gauge.

The southbound *Trans Karoo* Express, Johannesburg to Cape Town, changed engines at Kimberley where the electrified section from Jo'burg ends and steam took over for the trip to Beaufort West, from where the line was electrified to Cape Town. A class 25NC waits to depart with a rake of classic southern African clerestory coaches in September 1968.

Bloemfontein shed was one of the largest on SAR, serving a crossroads on the system with major routes in all four directions. In September 1968 the allocation of 175 included all six class 16E pacifics, 97 class 23 4-8-2s, and 18 class 19D 2-8-2s. There were also a number of older classes including six class 8 4-8-0s mainly used for shunting. The shed looks very tidy on 26th September 1968.

At the time of the RCTS railtour the Johannesburg to Bloemfontein line was still steam south of Kroonstad. Having crossed the Modder River north of Bloemfontein the line climbed steeply to a summit at Karee. Just below the summit a kopee (hillock) provided a superb vantage point to photograph the endless procession of trains coming up the bank. Bloemfontein had been requested to use a variety of engines on the trains, most of which were doubleheaded, to make sure they were clean and for the crews to produce smoke. Here a class 16DA 4-6-2, No.878, pilots a class 15F 4-8-2 on a northbound freight, much of which is obscured by the smoke on 26th September 1968.

There were no preserved railways in southern Africa in April 1971. The Gwelo & District Light Railway operated a 2 ft gauge line on former Rhodesia Railways land near Gwelo (Gweru) station. Built by enthusiasts, many of whom were RR employees, it operated one Sunday a month for visitors over a dumbell shaped layout, giving a continuous run of just under a mile. The two locomotives had come from the Selukwe Peak Light Railway, a mineral line south of Gwelo. *Buckeye* was built by Orenstein and Koppel in 1934.

Rhodesia Railways 15th class No.385, a 4-6-4 + 4-6-4 Garratt built by Beyer Peacock in 1949, takes water at Inseza with the Bulawayo to Salisbury (Harare) mixed in the late afternoon in March 1971. My trip had been arranged by Tony Baxter, deputy Chief Engineer of RR. After riding the engine to Gwelo we spent the night in his saloon, which was attached at the rear of the train, and included a bath. The mixed was normally worked by a hired SAR class 15E but it had been decreed that I should ride on a RR engine, hence No.385. Although beautifully cleaned externally, they had not cleaned the tubes and it struggled up the bank towards Somubula, west of Gwelo, with both pressure and water falling.

Modern Images

Most of the pictures in this book are of working railways. However, in recent years photographic charter trains have been organised where a group charter a train and take it out along the line, usually a preserved or heritage railway, and have run-pasts to take photographs. In addition, there are usually attempts to re-create scenes from the past.

Right: The Corris Railway (CR) closed in 1948 and its remaining stock of wagons and locomotives were acquired by the Talyllyn Railway. A section of the line, from the locomotive shed at Maespoeth to Corris has been rebuilt by a preservation group and a replica of loco No.4 built. Here this engine, numbered 7, approaches Corris station with a goods train comprising both restored original CR wagons and some replicas. A cameo is created with an Austin Seven and its suitably attired passengers watch as the train runs in.

Left: The National Tramway Museum at Crich has a large collection of restored trams and has also created a town street scene within which to run them. The site was originally a quarry with a mineral railway running to the lime works at Ambergate. On closure the Talyllyn Railway contracted to lift the mineral line and reuse the rails at Tywyn. My first working party for the TR was at Crich in 1958 and the combination of this link, and an interest in trams, means I have made many visits. A night scene is created for a photographic charter using two Leeds Corporation trams posed in the street at Crich.

Above: Many of the narrow gauge lines in the British Isles have been closed and lost and one of the saddest was the Lynton & Barnstaple Railway (L&BR), closed by the Southern Railway in 1935. An enthusiast group has acquired part of the trackbed, including the station at Woody Bay and has relaid a section of track. None of the Lynton engines survived but another group, based on the Ffestiniog Railway (FR), have built a replica of *Lew*, the last engine constructed for the L&BR in 1925. It is called *Lyd*, perpetuating the L&BR practice of naming its locomotives after Devon rivers with three letter names. Normally based at Porthmadog it made a visit to the L&BR together with two FR coaches on 28th September 2010, and is seen approaching Woody Bay. The leading coach is the rebuilt L&BR coach formerly at Snapper. The loco has two cab roofs, one has the proper L&BR profile and the other, slightly lower and seen here, to fit the FR loading gauge. When viewed in black and white (see right) this scene looks like the L&BR in its independent days. *Lyd* has now been painted in Southern Railway (SR) green and numbered E190, the number it would have carried if the SR had acquired another locomotive for the L&BR.

The Ffestiniog Railway has restored its historic fleet of locomotives and coaches to a very high standard, and also built replicas of items which have been scrapped in the past. Here Double-Fairlie *Merddyn Emrys*, climbs the spiral out of Dduallt with a train of vintage coaches and a rake of empty slate wagons on the rear. The leading four wheeled coach is a replica, as is the fourth vehicle, the 'curly roofed' brake van. The spiral was built to complete the route back to Blaenau after the original route north of the Moelwyn tunnel was lost when the pump storage scheme reservoir at Tan-y-Grisiau flooded the alignment.

The Isle of Man Railway has seen varied fortunes since the the former company closed the line in 1965, but is now in excellent condition. A double-headed photographic charter train passes Keristal, at the summit of the climb out of Douglas on 16th April 2012. There have been varied liveries since 1965 but by 2012 most of the stock was in the post war Isle of Man Railway Company livery of Indian red engines and red and cream coaches. No.4 *Loch* pilots No.13 *Kissack*, on a seven coach train. The four leading coaches are the saloon carriages built in 1905. Not greatly used in former times as their seating capacity is less than the compartment stock, they look more modern, not having continuous footboards. A 1959 Austin-Healey Sprite poses on the road. Up until 1939 the standard gauge Douglas Head Marine Drive tramway ran along the left hand side of the road, which has since been widened.

The Manx Electric Railway is timeless with both rolling stock and the scenery not changing much in the last 100 or more years, though the state of the track has varied and is now in much better condition than it has been for many years. No.7 dates from 1894 and has recently been repainted in the blue and white livery believed to be the original colours. It is lettered Douglas & Laxey Electric Tramway. The lettering on the vehicles changed frequently in the first 10 years of the line's operation, until it became bankrupt in 1902 and was bought by the Manx Electric Railway Company, who ran the system until it was taken over by the Manx government in 1957. No.7 and its matching trailer are approaching Brown's Crossing at the head of Glen Mona.

The Welsh Highland Railway opened in 1923, the culmination of numerous attempts to connect the North Wales Narrow Gauge Railway, from Dinas Junction, south of Caernarfon and Rhyd Ddu at the foot of Snowdon, to Porthmadog. It had a short and unhappy life, closing to passengers in 1936 and to freight the following year, being lifted for scrap during World War II.

There were various schemes to re-open the line and this was eventually achieved when the railway was re-opened between Caernarvon and Porthmadog in 2011. It is operated by the Ffestiniog Railway and the service trains use modern coaches hauled by ex-South African NGG 16 Garratts. The scenic highlight is the Pass of Aberglaslyn, south of Beddgelert and here *Merddyn Emrys,* one of the FR's Double-Fairlies, with a train of FR stock behind, heads a photographic special southbound through the pass and into the long tunnel. The river Glaslyn is at the bottom left.

Many derelict locos and vehicles have been restored to pristine condition. The restoration of a Great Western Railway (GWR) steam railcar is one of the more unusual feats. Steam railcars had a relatively short lifespan. The GWR ones disappeared in the 1930s with many being converted to auto trailers and the last, former Lancashire & Yorkshire Railway and London and North Western Railway units, were withdrawn after WWII. Therefore, the restoration of GWR No.93 by the Great Western Society (GWS) enables people to see, and experience, a type of rail travel few alive today can remember. Much of the work was carried out at Llangollen and before the railcar was taken to the GWS site at Didcot it ran a few trips on the Llangollen Railway, including a couple of days of charters. It is seen in this photograph as it approaches Glyndyfrdwy from Llangollen on 22nd March 2011. An unusual sight of a carriage with steam coming from it.

Shed Scenes

On 3rd April 1965 in the yard outside the shed at York, engine ash is dropped and locos, some having worked into York from other sheds, are prepared. Here class K1 2-6-0 No.62005 stands next to class A1 No.60152 *Holyrood*, with a class B1 in the background. The K1 has been preserved, and is now owned by the North Eastern Locomotive Preservation Group. Having recently had a major overhaul, it will be working the *Jacobite* steam trains from Fort William to Mallaig during 2012.

In the roundhouse at York, now the National Railway Museum, two class A1s, No.60150 *Willbrook* and No. 60121 *Silurian* simmer gently, while an unidentified class V2 stands on the right and No.43076, an Ivatt class 4MT, stands on the left on 2nd May 1965. There was always something special about a loco shed, with the warmth of engines in steam and the gentle noises of steam and water drifting from valves and cocks.

Adelaide shed was the Great Northern Railway (Ireland) (GNR(I)) shed in Belfast, and by July 1965 steam was near the end. The Derry line had closed and only the main line to Dublin remained. GNR(I) 4-4-0 No.171, *Slieve Gullion*, is a class S locomotive introduced in 1913. Along with the other class S engines it was renewed in 1938 with new frames and boilers. When the GNR(I) was split between the Córas Iompair Éireann (CIE) and the Ulster Transport Authority (UTA) in 1958, No.171 passed to CIE who withdrew it in January 1963. It was bought, along with several other engines, by UTA in June 1963 and saw further service until Autumn 1965. It was handed to the Railway Preservation Society of Ireland in January 1966 and has since worked railtours on the main line at various times. On the left is UTA No.56, a 2-6-4T. Known as 'Jeeps' they were based on the LMS Fowler 2-6-4T, and were built at Derby between 1947 and 1950. They were then delivered in pieces and assembled in Belfast. No.56 was one of the last batch. With reduced work on the former Northern Counties Committee (NCC) lines several were transferred to the GNR(I) section in 1958. No.56 was transferred back to York Road to work the spoil trains along the Larne line. It was withdrawn in April 1969 and scrapped in October 1970.

Skipton shed was alongside the goods yard to the west of the station, a brick and concrete structure built in the early 1950s when the previous wooden building became too dilapidated. It closed in April 1967, just over a year after this picture was taken in January 1966. It was then largely home to standard class 4MT 4-6-0s. No.75019 was a regular performer on the Grassington (Swinden) lime trains, working until mid 1968.

Jubilee class 4-6-0 No.45562 *Alberta* is serviced at Kingmoor shed, Carlisle on 7th October 1967 while working a Jubilee Society special, *South Yorkshireman No.8* Railtour from Bradford Exchange to Carlisle via Manchester, Preston and Shap. It will return with the railtour to Leeds via Ais Gill, and the train will be taken on to Bradford by sister engine No.45593 *Kolhapur*. The last *Jubilees* were based at Holbeck shed in Leeds and were used on a number of railtours.

The last night of BR steam. Well almost as this picture was taken about midnight on Saturday 3rd August 1968. At this point the last steam hauled service trains have run, although there would be a number of specials the following day and the famous 15 guinea specials on 11th August. At Lostock Hall shed, Preston, Black Five No.44806 drops its fire. It is now preserved at the Llangollen Railway.

Class 4MT 4-6-0 No.75014 has steam to spare as it passes through the deep cutting at Talerddig Summit with the up *Cambrian Coast Express* at Easter 1965. The *Manors* which had handled the express for many years have given way to BR standard engines, which would work the train till its withdrawal in March 1967.

Coming Soon From Holne Publishing

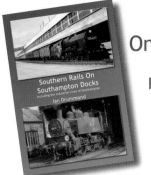

Southern Rails On Southampton Docks
Including the Industrial Railways of Southampton
By Ian Drummond

Rails Along The Derwent:
The Story of the Derwent Valley Light Railway
By Jonathan Stockwell and Ian Drummond
(Due July 2013)

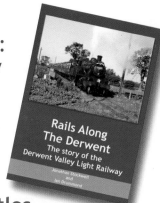

Previous Titles

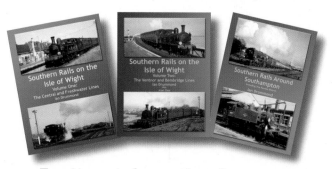

For More Information Contact:
Holne Publishing, PO Box 343, Leeds, LS19 9FW
enquiries@holnepublishing.co.uk
www.holnepublishing.co.uk